GREAT BOOK OF
MAGIC

Peter Eldin

BARRON'S

First edition for the United States, its territories and possessions, and Canada published in 2008 by Barron's Educational Series, Inc.

All inquiries should be addressed to:
Barron's Educational Series, Inc.
250 Wireless Blvd.
Hauppauge, NY 11788
www.barronseduc.com

ISBN-13: 978-0-7641-6174-2
Library of Congress Catalog No.: 2007942125

Manufactured by: Sun Power Printing Co. Ltd., Dongguan, China
Date of Manufacture: July 2014
9 8 7 6

A HALDANE MASON BOOK
Art Director: Ron Samuel
Artwork: Peter Bull Studio
Picture acknowledgements: **Edwin A. Dawes Collection:** 4, 5, 10, 12, 14, 16, 20, 22, 24, 26, 30, 32, 34, 36, 40, 42, 44, 46; **Corbis:** 6

CONTENTS

WELCOME 4
Dos and Don'ts 6
Hints and Tips 8

PERFORMING CLOSE-UP 9
Money Magic 10
Conjuring with Cards 12
Oriental Wizardry 14
Crazy Compass 16
Traveling Coin 18

CLASSICS OF MAGIC 19
Carmo's Beads 20
An Amazing Production 22
Chameleon Colors 24
Magic Washing 26
Ball and Vase 28

MAGIC OF THE MIND 29
Dice Deception 30
Telephone Telepathy 32
Open Sesame 34
Looking into the Future 36
The Dictionary Test 38

LADIES OF LEGERDEMAIN .. 39
Afghan Bands 40
Floating on Air 42
Show of Strength 44
Wave the Flag 46

INDEX 48

WELCOME . . .

. . . to the wonderful world of magic. We live in a fantastic technological age, where amazing things happen at the touch of a button. And yet people are still amused, entertained, and amazed at the skill of a magician. This is true all over the world, for magic as entertainment appeals to people of all ages and all nationalities.

The same is true of magic as a hobby. It is a fascinating hobby that can bring you fun and a great deal of pleasure, no matter what your age or sex. Being able to do magic is a great confidence-builder. People who can do even just a few magic tricks are generally much more confident than those who can't, because they become used to appearing before and talking with groups of people of all ages.

Learning magic also improves your mind, makes you more alert, and gives you self-esteem.

Please do not think that just by reading this book you will become a magician. This book is just the start. To be successful, you must work at it and do your utmost to make your magic entertaining, not just a mechanical and boring demonstration.

Many of the big names in magic used beautifully colored posters to publicize their shows. Some of them are now sold for large sums of money.

There are lots of other books on magic that will teach you more tricks and help you develop into a competent magician. Magic is one of those subjects that is never ending but endlessly fascinating. Read as much as you can about magic and magicians.

Many magicians have been studying all their lives and yet still do not know it all. But, they continue to learn all the time. The study of magic is an endless road with exciting new discoveries at every bend.

With this book you may have taken your first step on a journey into wonderment, excitement, and fascination. Welcome to the wonderful world of magic!

The poster opposite shows Okito with one of his famous illusions: a ball that floated in the air. Thurston's poster below provides insight into the many wonders in store for the audience.

DOs AND DON'Ts

There are two really important rules about performing magic that you need to be aware of. The first is advance preparation—making, buying, or preparing the various items required. The second is practicing the trick until you can do it without thinking about the various movements involved. The actual mechanics of most tricks are really quite simple, and many tricks are quite easy to do. But even the simplest of tricks must be practiced if you want to give a performance that both you and your audience will enjoy.

DOs

- Always practice any trick before showing it to anyone. This means that you must perform it in private over and over again, until the actions become automatic and you do not have to stop and think what you have to do. This will also help you uphold the Magician's Oath, never to reveal your magic secrets.

- After practice come rehearsals, when you perform the trick, still in private, exactly as if you were performing for a

Magic can be performed almost anywhere. Magicians not only work in theaters or on television; many perform at private parties, and some travel the world entertaining audiences on cruise ships. But wherever they perform, magicians are usually well dressed.

THE MAGICIAN'S OATH

Professional magicians often swear an oath not to reveal how tricks are done, either by telling someone or by doing the trick clumsily and thus revealing the method. The Oath goes something like this:

"As a magician, I promise never to reveal the secret of any trick to a non-magician unless he or she swears to uphold the Magician's Oath in turn. I promise never to perform any trick for any non-magician without first practicing it thoroughly until I can perform it well enough to maintain the illusion of magic."

With this in mind, make sure you practice enough so that you can perform your tricks seamlessly and not reveal any of your secrets!

real audience. This means that every word you say and every movement you make must be the same as those of an actual show.

- Always be well dressed and well groomed when performing. When you are in front of an audience, all attention will be on you, so you should look the best you possibly can. You don't have to have a special suit or wear a top hat, but clothes should be clean and pressed, shoes should be polished, hair should be tidy, and your hands must be clean.

- Always appear enthusiastic and happy when performing. If you are happy, this feeling will be transferred to the audience and they will enjoy your show even more. So will you.

DON'Ts
- Never be rude or offensive to anyone in your audience—even those who may be trying to make fun of you.
- Never tell anyone, except another magician, how the tricks are done.

HINTS AND TIPS

Here are some useful hints and tips to help you get the best out of your magic.

Watch yourself

A camcorder is a great way to watch your performance from the audience's viewpoint. It will let you see any mistakes you are making, and will help you spot any areas that need improvement.

Practice makes perfect

Never perform a trick for anyone until you have practiced it well. You must know exactly what you are doing so you can concentrate on entertaining the audience rather than just demonstrating a trick.

Less is more

If you show more than one trick, do not go over the top and perform everything you can. Two or three tricks at a time is enough for anybody—and you will always have other tricks that you can show at another time.

Once is enough!

Never perform the same trick twice in quick succession. If you are good, people may ask to see the trick again. Do not fall into this trap—show them another trick instead. If you do the trick again, someone in the audience will be more likely to work out how you did it.

Keep it fun

Remember that it is fun to fool an audience, but not to make fools of them. Your job as a magician is to entertain, not to prove how clever you are.

Prepare properly

Some of the tricks in this book need some secret preparation beforehand. Always do this preparation in private.

Patter is important

Most of your tricks will require you to do some talking. Magicians call this talking "patter." Patter must be practiced as much as the actual trick so you know exactly what you are going to say, when you are going to say it, and how you are going to say it. It may seem like hard work, but you will find it well worthwhile to actually write out your patter so you do not say anything silly, superfluous, or repetitive. Writing it out is also a useful means of correcting your patter and honing it to be as good as you can possibly make it.

PERFORMING CLOSE-UP

Most new magicians get their first experience of performing by doing tricks for family and friends seated around a table. This is known as "close-up magic." There are many magicians who do close-up professionally, working in restaurants, trade shows, and at events such as weddings or parties.

Close-up magic can be performed with objects that you have in your pockets, or even with things your audience has in their pockets or purses. Alternatively, if you are asked in advance to perform a small show of close-up magic, you can prepare with slightly bigger things and carry them around in a small case.

Close-up is a fascinating area of magic. Most people have not seen a magic act live, and they are doubly amazed that you can fool and entertain them right in front of their very eyes!

You will need:
- *thick cloth to put on your table*
- *the coin box provided*
- *handkerchief*

MONEY MAGIC

Polish-born Max Malini performed close-up magic for commoners and kings. Born Max Katz Breit in Ostrov, Poland in 1873, his family emigrated to America when he was quite young. By the time he was 15 he was a professional magician. Originally he performed in bars, but later he sold tickets for private shows in hotel rooms. He performed for many rich people, including American presidents and European monarchs.

Most of Malini's magic was done with everyday objects, with his audience close to him. Sometimes he would approach a famous person and bite a button from their clothing, and then use his magic to restore it to its proper place!

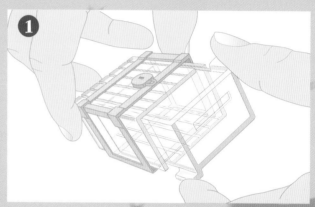

1 *Examine your box in private before the show. Look carefully at the end with the coin slot. Use your index finger and thumb to hold the top right and bottom left corners of the box and pull gently. This will open the secret drawer that slides inside the outer box. Practice opening and closing the box until you can do it quickly with your eyes closed.*

2 *To perform the trick, show the closed coin box to the audience. Borrow a coin from a spectator and drop it into the box. Use either a nickel or dime.*

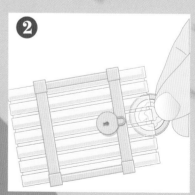

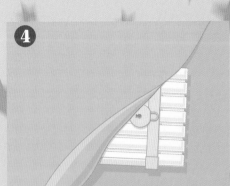

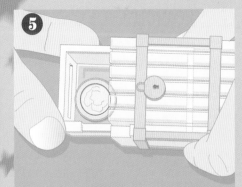

3 Pretend that you are unable to get the coin out of the box to return it to the spectator. You may like to ask one or two members of the audience if they can open the box —but don't let them examine it for too long, in case they discover your secret!

4 Say that you are going to have to use magic to free the trapped coin from the box. Put the box upside down on top of the thick cloth on your table, and continue to hold it while you ask a spectator to cover it with the handkerchief.

5 As the handkerchief is being placed over the box, quickly open it, tip the coin out on to the thick cloth (this will cover the sound of the coin falling out on to the table), and then close the box. Remove your hands from under the handkerchief. Now wave your wand over the handkerchief and mutter some magic words.

6 Ask a spectator to remove the handkerchief. The coin is seen to have escaped from the box and is on the table.

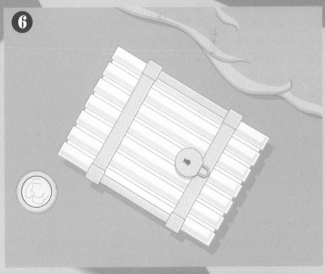

You will need:
• a deck of cards

CONJURING WITH CARDS

Cardini was born Richard Valentine Pitchford in Wales in 1895. He practiced his magic in the trenches of the First World War and then in a hospital after he was injured in battle.

After the war he performed in top theaters in all parts of the world. One unusual aspect of Cardini's act was that he wore white gloves, which made his sleight of hand manipulations even more difficult. Part of his success stemmed from the fact that he did not appear as a magician, but as someone to whom amazing things happened without him knowing quite how or why. He adopted the name Cardini because much of his act consisted of producing fans of playing cards from thin air.

To produce fans of cards from nowhere, as Cardini did, requires a lot of practice. However, there are some slightly easier tricks with cards that can be performed, such as this one.

❶

1   Hand the deck to a spectator and ask him/her to shuffle the cards.

❷

2   Take back the cards and spread them face up between your hands to show they are well mixed. What you are really doing is memorizing the card at the right end of the spread, which will be on the bottom of the pack when you put it down.

3 Turn the pack face down and spread them out again as you ask someone to take any card.

4 Ask the spectator to show the card to the rest of the audience, taking care not to let you see it.

5 Ask the spectator to memorize the card, and then to replace it face down on top of the deck.

6 Take the bottom half of the deck and place it on top so the chosen card is lost somewhere in the center of the deck. This is called "cutting the cards," and you can do it several times to ensure that the cards really are mixed up.

7 Now spread out the cards with the faces toward you, and take out the card that is to the right of the card you remembered earlier—this will be the card chosen by the spectator.

8 Ask the spectator for the name of the card he/she chose. Slowly turn over the card you are holding —it is the very same card!

ORIENTAL WIZARDRY

Although the magician Okito performed in Chinese costume, he was actually Dutch and his real name was Tobias "Theo" Leendert Bamberg. He was born in Holland in 1875, the son of David Tobias Bamberg, who was the court magician to King William III. Okito was the sixth consecutive generation of magicians, and his son David (who performed as Fu Manchu) followed him into the family profession.

Okito always performed silently, as he was extremely deaf following a swimming accident. He became very popular in Holland before going on to tour the world with a spectacular and colorful show.

This trick—a very old one that used to be called "Buddha Papers"—can be presented as a Chinese trick if you decorate the papers appropriately (see the last step opposite for ideas).

14

You will need:
- *2 sheets of paper, about a 5 inch (12 cm) square*
- *glue*
- *an unusual coin*

1

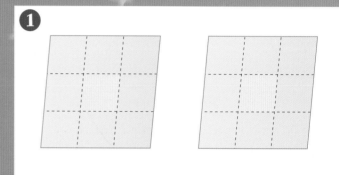

1 *Fold each sheet into nine equal sections and open them out again. The folds should be in the same position as the dotted lines shown here.*

2

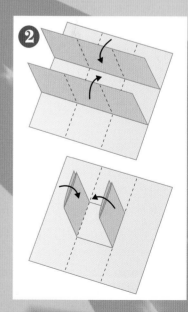

2 *Place one sheet of paper on top of the other and glue them together at the center (as shown by the shading in step 1). Do the folding and gluing really neatly, and then close up each sheet into a little packet.*

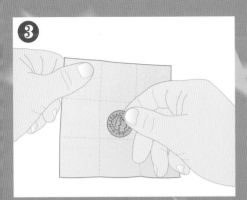

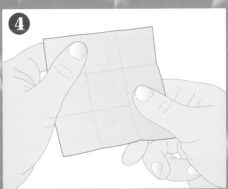

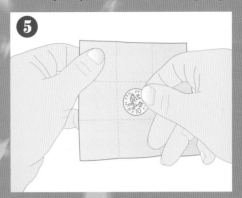

3 Open out the top sheet and place the unusual coin in the center. Fold the paper over the coin, from the top and bottom, and then in from each side. Turn the whole thing over. Now you are ready to begin the trick.

4 Show your little packet (consisting of two folded sheets glued together in the center) to the audience, and open the empty side. Make sure it's the empty side you open!

5 Place a borrowed coin in the center of the paper and close to form a packet. As you do this, turn the packet over. It is a good idea to keep speaking directly to your audience during this movement, so that everyone will be looking at you and not at your hands.

6 Wave your hand over the packet and carefully open the top side of the packet. Of course, the coin revealed will be completely different.

By doing the same moves again, you can change this coin back into the one you have just borrowed.

If you are using an oriental-looking coin, it is a good idea to decorate the sheets of paper with oriental symbols. If you are using a different coin, use other signs, such as signs of the Zodiac. But both sheets must be decorated identically, or it will soon become obvious that there is more than one packet.

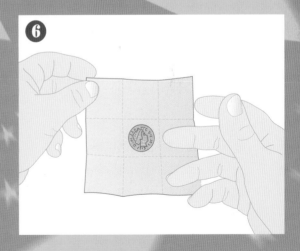

CRAZY COMPASS

You will need:
- *piece of thick black card*
- *white, silver, or gold pen or paint*
- *pencil*
- *scissors*

When he was just seven years of age, Howard Thurston saw a performance by the magician Herrmann the Great and immediately decided that he, too, wanted to be a magician.

He started his magical career in an American circus, followed by appearances in carnivals. Then he graduated to the theater. Initially, he specialized in magic with cards, and made a big impression on theater audiences when he appeared in London in 1900. Howard Thurston eventually developed a large-scale illusion act that he toured the world with before returning to America, where he became the most famous magician in the country, remaining so for over thirty years.

This magic compass would have been of no use to Thurston on his world tours, as it keeps changing direction!

1   Cut an octagonal (8-sided) shape from the card. This should be small enough for you to hold it on edge between your thumb and index finger. Draw an arrow pointing vertically on one side of the octagon. Turn the octagon over and draw an arrow horizontally, so that the two arrows are at right angles to each other.

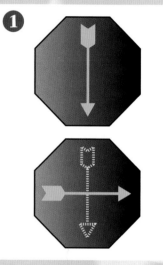

❶

2   To perform the trick, hold the compass in your left hand between the thumb and index finger so that the arrow is at a 45° angle as shown here.

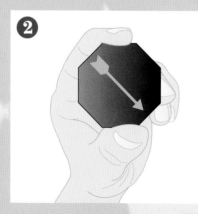

❷

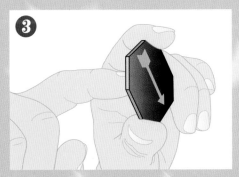

3 With your right index finger, gently push on the rear right edges of the compass to turn it around to show the other side. The arrows will point in the same direction. Turn the compass a couple more times to emphasize the fact that the arrows on each side are pointing the same way.

4 Now move the compass so that the arrow is pointing downwards. Turn the compass in the same way as before—the arrow on the other side is pointing to the right.

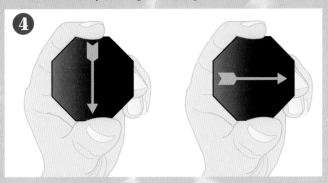

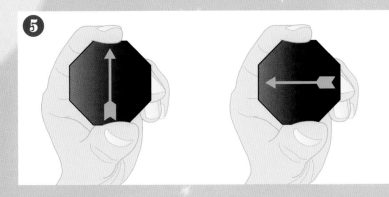

5 Reposition the compass in your fingers so the arrow is pointing upwards. When you turn the compass this time, one arrow points upwards and the other points to the left.

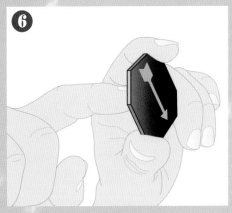

6 Move the compass back to its original position (as in step 2), and turn it to show the arrows pointing the same way once again.

You will need:
• *two coins*

TRAVELING COIN

①

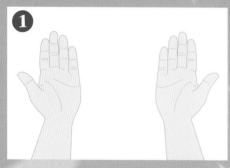

1 Rest your hands, palms up, flat on a table. They should be about 5 in (12 cm) apart.

②

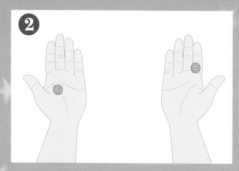

2 Put one coin on your left hand and the other on your right as shown. The positioning of these two coins is important.

③

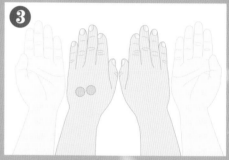

3 Quickly turn both hands inwards and over simultaneously. As you do so, the coin in your right hand will fly over to the left so that it ends up under your left hand.

④

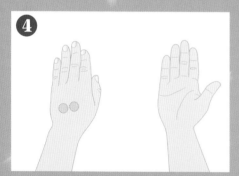

4 Pause for a second or two and slowly lift your right hand. The coin has disappeared!

⑤

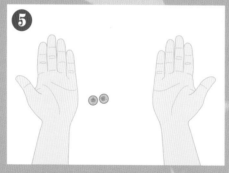

5 Now lift your left hand and let everyone see that the two coins have now come together by magic.

This trick works by itself because of the positioning of the coins. But, you still need to practice it carefully before you show it to anyone to make sure you do it right every time.

If you are left-handed, you may find that the trick works better if the positioning of the coins is switched.

CLASSICS OF MAGIC

Some tricks are known to magicians as "Classics of Magic," for they are as popular today as when they were first invented. Often such tricks are quite old, but they have stood the test of time and remained popular with audiences.

One of the most notable of all the classics is the "cups and balls" trick. In this trick, small balls appear, disappear, and multiply beneath three cups. It was known to the Romans and is described in the first books published about magic, but it is still performed to this day. Another classic is cutting a rope in two and restoring it to one piece. And there is the "linking rings" trick in which metal rings link and unlink inexplicably.

Not all the classics are old. Some new tricks quickly become regarded as classics. This is simply due to the fact that audiences love seeing them. But even a classic depends for its success upon the way that the magician performs it. The tricks on the following pages are not particularly old, but they can be regarded as classics. Remember that it is still up to you as a performer to make them entertaining so that your audience can really enjoy them.

CARMO'S BEADS

You will need:
- *15–20 beads*
- *thick thread*
- *a small glass*
- *scissors*

The Australian magician Carmo performed mainly in the circus. His name lives on in the history of magic for one particular trick, known as Carmo's Beads. In this trick, beads cut from a necklace are magically re-strung.

Carmo, whose real name was Henry Cameron, began his performing career as a strong man, juggler, and contortionist until he moved to England in 1910, when he became a magician. He toured with his own circus, "The Great Carmo Circus and Menagerie," until the circus was destroyed by fire in 1930. After his death in 1944, his wife Rita, who had been Carmo's assistant, carried on with her own magic act.

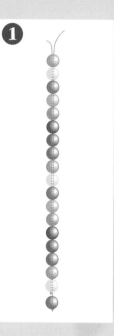

1   *Before your show, thread the beads with two threads. One thread goes through all of the beads, and the other goes through all but the last one.*

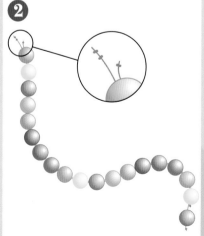

2   *So you know which thread is which, tie a single knot in the end of the shorter thread that does not go through the last bead, and two knots in the end of the long thread that goes through all the beads.*

3   To perform the trick, make sure
    you hold the thread with two
    knots. Hold up the necklace
    of beads and show it to
    your audience. Put the
    glass under the necklace.

4   Take the scissors and cut through the
    thread above the bottom bead. All
    the beads will slide off the thread
    into the glass. It looks as if the beads
    are now all separate, but of course
    they are still joined together by the
    shorter thread.
        Pretend to drop the loose thread
    into the glass, but secretly keep it
    in your hand.

5   Wave your wand over the glass and
    then pull out the beads, which are now
    magically threaded into one long necklace
    again. (There will be one bead still in the
    glass, but no one will notice that.)

AN AMAZING PRODUCTION

You will need:
- *table with a cloth*
- *2 safety pins*
- *piece of material 20 in (50 cm) square*
- *4 plastic or metal rings large enough to put your thumb into*
- *peg*
- *scarves and ribbons*
- *small toy rabbit*
- *cardboard box about 10 in (25 cm) square*
- *magic wand*

John Henry Anderson of Scotland, the Great Wizard of the North, was born at Craigmyle, near Aberdeen, in 1814. He wanted to be an actor, but after seeing a magician perform he changed his mind and took up magic instead.

His equipment was always the finest he could afford, and he constantly introduced new and spectacular tricks to his repertoire during his tours of Britain, America, and Europe. He was one of the first to realize that good publicity can bring audiences in to see shows. It is believed that he was the first magician to produce a rabbit from a hat.

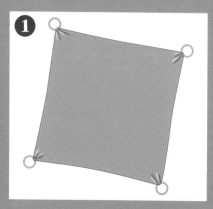

1   *Before your show, sew the rings on to each corner of the material.*

2   *Use the safety pins to pin up the back of the tablecloth (the side that will be away from your audience) as shown.*

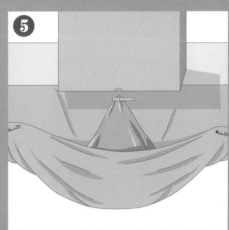

3 Put the toy rabbit, the scarves, and the ribbons onto the center of the square of material. Then bring the four rings together to form a bag, and secure it with the peg.

4 Place the bag into the fold of the tablecloth and put the box on the table, with the open side facing the audience.

5 To perform the trick, lift up the box and wave your free hand inside it to emphasize that it is empty. Turn the box over so that the opening is at the bottom, and put it back on the table so that it overlaps the back of the table a little.

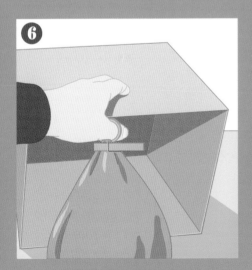

6 Tap the bottom of the box with your magic wand to show that it is solid. As you lift the box to tap the sides, slip your thumb through the rings so that as you tip the box forward to tap the sides, the secret bundle falls inside the box.

7 Place the box back on the table with the open side up. Reach into the box, quickly undo the peg, and pull forth the ribbons and scarves and then the toy rabbit.

23

CHAMELEON COLORS

Ade Duval was born Adolph Amrein in the American city of Cincinnati on December 31, 1898. He became interested in magic after seeing Howard Thurston, and made his first appearance in his late teens. Initially, he worked a double act with another magician, but eventually he became a solo performer.

With his wife True as his assistant, Duval presented an act using a multitude of colored handkerchiefs (magicians call them "silks"), which had the title "A Rhapsody in Silk." He was a big success in American vaudeville and also appeared in Europe and Australia. Ade Duval invented many magic tricks, but the most famous was one in which white handkerchiefs changed color when pushed through a simple cardboard tube.

You will need:

- cardboard tube about 6 in (15 cm) long and big enough to fit over your thumb
- short strip of material 1 in (2 cm) wide
- sticky tape and elastic band
- 2 different colored silk handkerchiefs (one red and one blue, for example)
- 2 white silk handkerchiefs
- sheet of paper, standard size
- magic wand from your box

1 Before your show, cut two horizontal slits on each side of the middle of the tube and thread the strip of material through them. Use the sticky tape to hold the strip in place. The strip should be long enough to hang down almost to the end of the tube.

2 Push the two colored handkerchiefs and then one white one into the tube until the strip of material stops you from pushing any further.

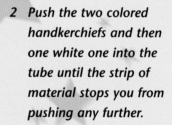

3 Put the stiff paper on your table, and put the tube beneath it on the right-hand side near the end of the paper furthest from the audience.

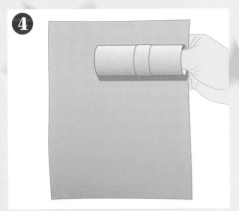

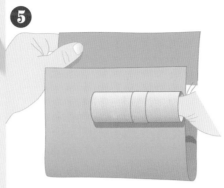

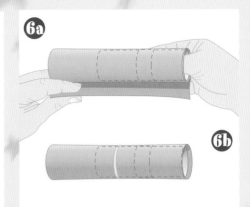

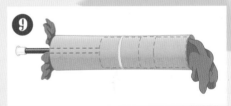

4 To show the trick, pick up the paper with both hands. At the same time, push your right thumb into the tube so it stays hidden behind the paper.

5 With your left hand, take the bottom of the paper away from you up to your right fingers, which take it. The edge that was being held by the right hand is allowed to drop down so that the audience has seen both sides of the paper, but the tube has remained hidden.

6 With your left hand, roll the paper around your right thumb (and the hidden tube). Use both hands to roll the paper up to make a long tube with the small tube hidden inside. Use the elastic band to hold this in place.

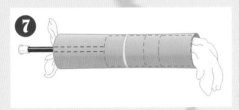

7 Take your second white handkerchief and push it into the left end of the long tube. Use your wand to push the white handkerchief right through the tube. What actually happens is the white handkerchief placed in the small tube earlier is pushed out, and it appears that the handkerchief has gone right through the tube.

8 Take the white handkerchief and push it into the left end of the tube as before. This time, the wand pushes out the red handkerchief, and it seems that the white one has changed color. When showing this trick, use your wand to make sure the handkerchiefs are pushed securely into the small tube.

9 Finally, put the red handkerchief into the tube in the same way. It comes out blue!

You now allow the small tube holding the handkerchiefs to slip out of the long tube, taking care to drop it behind something on your table. Hold up the long tube to show your audience it is empty.

You will need:
- *magic wand*
- *2 pieces of soft cord each at least 6.5 ft (2 m) long*
- *4 silk handkerchiefs*

MAGIC WASHING

Dante was born August Harry Jansen on October 3, 1883, in Denmark. His family moved to America when he was six years old. He became interested in magic after seeing the great magician, Alexander Herrmann. Dante began by building equipment for magicians. When

he started performing himself, he was chosen by Howard Thurston to run one of his illusion shows with which he toured the world.

To magicians, the most famous trick performed by Dante was one he performed sitting on a chair with two assistants doing all the work. In the trick, handkerchiefs and Dante's cane magically freed themselves from tied ropes. This trick, which is very old, used to be known to magicians as "Cords of Phantasia." Now it is usually called "Magic Washing."

1 *Invite two people to come up and help you as you drape the cords over the wand. One person can hold the wand.*

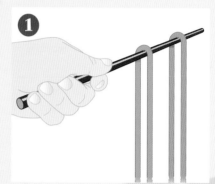

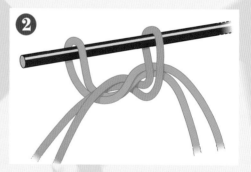

2 *Hold the two ends of one cord in one hand and the two ends of the second cord in the other hand. Tie the ropes together with a single knot around the wand as shown.*

Hand the two ends of the first cord to one person and the two ends of the second cord to the other person. The wand does not have to be held now that the ropes are tied around it.

3 Tie the four handkerchiefs around the cords, two on one side of the wand and two on the other. Push the handkerchiefs right up close to the wand.

4 Now ask each helper to hand one cord end to you. Tie them in a single knot and hand the ends back. (This means that you have actually changed the ends over.)

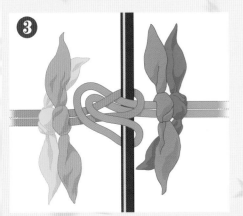

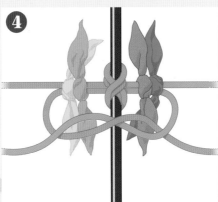

5 Get the helpers to tightly hold the cords, and then quickly pull out the wand. The handkerchiefs will fall off, and the helpers will be holding the cords between them. Note: If the handkerchiefs do not come off immediately, ask your helpers to give the cords a tug. This will help free them.

You will need:
• *the ball and vase trick from your box (it contains a cup, ball, secret section with dummy ball, and a lid)*

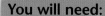

BALL AND VASE

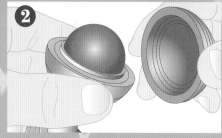

1   Before you perform this trick, take the real ball from the cup and place it into your left jacket pocket. Put the lid and the secret piece back on top of the vase.

2   Hold the ring forming the secret compartment with your left fingers, and lift the lid with your right hand. It looks as if there is a ball in the vase. Replace the lid.

3   Say you will make the ball vanish. Muttering magic words, wave your wand over the vase and lift the lid (and the secret portion) with your right hand. The vase is empty.

4   Holding the lid in your right hand, take the ball from your pocket with your left hand. The ball seems to have flown to your pocket by magic. Put the ball in the vase and replace the lid.

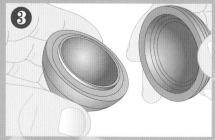

5   Use the third and fourth fingers of your left hand to pick up the vase by its stem, and lift off the lid with your right hand. Tip the ball into your open left hand, place the vase back on the table, and put the lid back on. Pretend to place the ball in your right hand, but secretly keep it hidden in your left.

6   Look at your right hand (which the spectators believe has the ball) as your left secretly drops the ball into your pocket. Pick up the vase with your left hand holding on to the secret section and take off the lid. The ball has returned to the vase by magic!

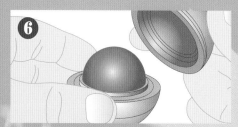

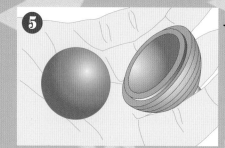

MAGIC OF THE MIND

Appearing to read the mind of a spectator, or transmitting thoughts by apparent telepathy, are the most intriguing types of magic. With normal conjuring, the audience knows that it must be a trick, even though they may not know how it is done. But with any magic of the mind, there is always a suspicion that these baffling feats could be real and not achieved by trickery.

Mind magic, or "mentalism" to magicians, covers a wide spectrum of different feats. Mentalists can appear to predict future events, read sealed messages, transmit their thoughts to others, or receive thoughts from their audience. Some mental effects give the appearance of willing a spectator to do something the magician wants. In others, the mentalist may show that he or she can identify objects held by spectators, even while blindfolded.

As a general rule, mental magicians do not claim any supernatural powers but allow spectators to make up their own minds as to whether the feats performed are tricks or not. In other words, the mentalist or mind magician demonstrates powers that seem superhuman to most people.

You will need:
- *three dice*
- *a pencil*
- *paper*

DICE DECEPTION

In the 1950s, Al Koran was Britain's best known magician specializing in magic of the mind. He was born Edward Doe in 1914, and became interested in magic after helping a street magician pack his bags. In return for this help, the performer taught Doe some of the classic tricks in magic.

At the start of his career, Al Koran specialized in close-up magic. Later, he concentrated on mental magic, although he continued to perform more conventional magic tricks as well. A big television star in Britain, in 1969 he decided to move to Chicago to try and make his name in America, but he died just a couple of years later.

1 Hand the dice, pencil, and paper to a spectator, and ask him or her to throw the dice a few times to make sure they are normal.

2 Turn your back and ask the spectator to throw the dice again. Then ask him or her to do some mental arithmetic, using the pen and paper if it helps.

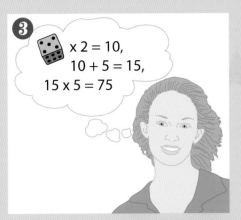

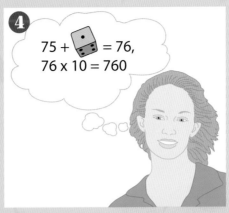

3   First, ask the spectator to multiply the number on the top of the first die by 2. Next, he or she is to add 5 to the answer and then multiply that answer by 5. For example, if the number is 5, then 5 x 2 = 10, 10 + 5 = 15, 15 x 5 = 75.

4   Now he or she has to add the number on the second die and multiply the resulting answer by 10. For example, if the second die shows a 1, then 75 + 1 = 76, and 76 x 10 = 760.

5   Finally, the number on the third die is added to the total and the spectator tells you what answer he or she has reached. For example, if the number on the third die is 4, then 760 + 4 = 764. The spectator gives you this number.

6   From this number, you then use your amazing mental powers to tell them the numbers on top of each of the three dice.

The secret is that you mentally subtract 250 from the answer you are given, and the answer you get is made up of the three numbers on top of the three dice. To continue our example, 764 – 250 = 514, the numbers on the three dice that you have not even seen!

TELEPHONE TELEPATHY

Husband and wife team Sydney and Lesley Piddington baffled the world with their feats of apparent telepathy, first on Australian radio and then, in 1949, on British radio. The two Australians seemed able to transmit thoughts between them even though they could be several miles apart.

Lesley could be in an airplane, a submarine, or even the Tower of London, but she was always correct in identifying a line from a book, a song title, or something similar chosen by someone in the radio studio and mentally transmitted to her by Sydney. They caused a sensation in Britain, and there were many theories as to how it was done. Was it all a trick, or was it actually genuine thought transference? The Piddingtons made only one comment: "You are the judge."

You will need:
- *a pack of cards*
- *a friend to help you*
- *a telephone*

❶

1 Show the cards, have them shuffled, and ask someone to pick any card and place it face up on the table. They have a completely free choice.
   Now say that you can transmit thoughts to your friend, and that you will give him or her a telephone call. Let's say her name is Anna.
   You ring Anna's number. When she answers, pretend that someone else has answered and say: "Could I speak to Anna, please?"

2 As soon as your Anna hears you, she starts to whisper the names of each card suit in turn: *"Clubs, diamonds, hearts, spades."* As soon as Anna mentions the suit of the chosen card, you say *"Thank you,"* as if the person to whom you are talking has gone to find Anna.

3 Anna now knows what suit has been chosen and needs to know the card's value or number. She does this in exactly the same way, by whispering each of the numbers in turn: *"Ace, two, three, four . . ."* up to *". . . jack, queen, king."* When the number of the chosen card is reached, pretend that Anna has only just come to the phone and say: *"Hello Anna, here is someone who wants to speak to you."* Anna now knows exactly what card was chosen.

4 Hand the telephone to one of the spectators. Anna tells them what card was selected as if you had transmitted this information to her by the power of your mind.

OPEN SESAME

You will need:
- a padlock
- 5 keys that look similar, but only one of them opens the padlock
- 5 envelopes

The American magician Ted Annemann was famous for his amazing feats of mind magic. He was born Theodore John Squires in East Waverley, New York, but was adopted by Stanley Anneman. Like many others before and since, he first learned magic from a magic set when he was 14. Four years later, he was a professional magician, adding an extra "n" to his surname.

He later decided to concentrate on magic of the mind. In 1934 he founded *The Jinx*, a magazine that was to become very influential in the world of magic. Although *The Jinx* ceased publication in 1941, magicians of today still use it as a reference work. A trick that Annemann often performed was the strangely named "Seven Keys to Baldpate," which used seven keys and a padlock. Here is a five-key version that you can do.

1 1 Before the start of your show, secretly mark one of the envelopes with a very small pencil dot.

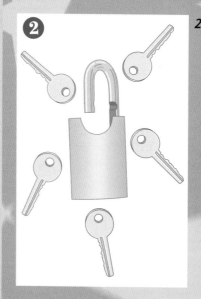

2 2 To perform the trick, show the padlock, the five keys, and the five envelopes spread out on your table. Ask a spectator to try a key in the padlock. You then pick up one of the envelopes and put the key into it. If it is the key that opens the lock, pick up the envelope with the pencil mark. If it doesn't open the lock, use one of the unmarked envelopes.

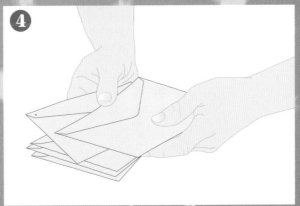

3   Keep doing this until all the keys have been tried and placed in the envelopes, which are sealed as you go along. Then hand all the envelopes to a spectator and ask him or her to mix them up so no one can know which envelope contains the only key that will open the lock.

4   Take the envelopes back and, while talking, casually place the marked envelope second from the top.

Hand the envelopes to someone and ask them to spell the word "magic," transferring one envelope to the bottom of the pile for each letter of the word. He or she then keeps the envelope that falls on the letter C and passes the remaining envelopes back to you.

5   This is repeated three more times until the fourth spectator hands you back the remaining envelope, which is the one marked with the small dot. Each person opens their envelope and tries the key in the padlock. None of them opens it—but the key in your envelope does!

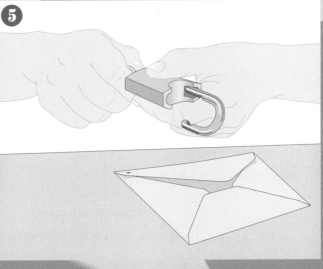

LOOKING INTO THE FUTURE

One of the most dynamic performers of mental magic was Maurice Fogel, whose feats of mind reading made headline news all over the world. He was born in London on July 7, 1911, and became interested in magic as a teenager when he read a magic book by Professor Hoffmann, a famous magical author.

After some performances at his school and a local youth club, he devised an act of magical impressions. He became a professional magician in 1937 when he won first prize in a talent competition. The shift to mental magic came when a show he was performing in proved to be too short and he was asked to devise an act to extend it. It was an important event that changed Fogel's life, for he came up with a mind-reading act and then went on to astound the world with his remarkable feats.

You will need:

- *3 pieces of card, small enough to fit into the envelope*
- *pencil*
- *envelope*
- *small piece of paper*

1

1   *Before your performance, draw a triangle on one card, a square on the second card and a circle on the third card. Write on the back of the triangle card: "You will choose this card." Write on the face of the envelope: "You will choose the square," and write on the piece of paper: "You will choose the circle." Put the piece of paper in the envelope.*

2   To perform the trick, show the three cards on
    your table while holding the envelope. Keep the
    paper hidden in the envelope, do not show the
    backs of the cards, and be careful not to show
    the front of the envelope.
       Ask someone to point to any one of the three
    designs. They have a perfectly free choice and
    can change their mind if they wish.

3   If the triangle is chosen, simply turn all three cards
    over to reveal the message. If the square is chosen,
    turn over the envelope. If the circle is chosen, reach
    into the envelope, take out the piece of paper, and
    show it to the audience.
       You have shown that you knew in advance what
    design would be chosen. But be careful when you
    put everything away—you don't want the unused
    messages to be seen.

You will need:
- *a dictionary*
- *a ballpoint pen or pencil*

THE·DICTIONARY·TEST

1   Go through the center portion of the dictionary, and write on the top corner of every right-hand page the word that is printed at the top of the left-hand page.

2   To perform the trick, open the book near the back, holding it in your right hand. With your left hand, flick the pages from the back of the book on to those at the rear. Ask someone to call out "stop" at any time as you do this.

3   Hold the book so the spectator can see and remember the word at the top of the left-hand page he or she stopped at, but not the right-hand page, which needs to be facing you. As the spectator is looking at the left-hand page, look down at the word you wrote on the opposite page. Close the book and then pretend to read the spectator's mind as you call out the mentally selected word letter by letter.

LADIES OF LEGERDEMAIN

Although magic is generally regarded as a male domain, there have been many successful female magicians. Some of the famous women who have performed magic through the ages began as assistants to male magicians, and many others were in some way related to a magician.

Okita, who was born Julia Ferrett in Britain, had a very successful act that she toured with through Britain and France. She performed in oriental style and was particularly well known for her presentation of the classic Linking Rings. Okita was taught by her husband, Charles De Vere, a popular British magician. Their daughter Ionia carried on the family tradition from 1910 with an illusion show that toured all over Europe. In 1917 she was caught up in the Russian Revolution, lost all her equipment, and had to hide in the cellar of her hotel for three months!

A famous female magician of the 20th century was Esme Levante, the daughter of illusionist The Great Levante. One of her specialities was to magically produce a live wallaby.

Today there are many outstanding female magicians performing all types of magic, from intimate close-up performances to large-scale illusion shows, and more and more are taking up magic as a hobby.

AFGHAN BANDS

After the death of magician Alexander Herrmann in 1896, his wife Adelaide, who had acted as his assistant, continued with the show to great acclaim. At first she performed with Alexander's nephew Leon Herrmann, but later set out on her own.

She was born Adelaide Scarcez, of Belgian parents, in London in 1853 and began her life as a professional dancer. She married Alexander in 1875 and he taught her how to do magic.

The Afghan Bands has been a popular trick since the time of Adelaide Herrmann, and may be even older. It was first called "The Afghan Bands" by Professor Hoffmann, who wrote many books on the art of magic.

1 *Prepare the three strips of paper by gluing the ends together to make three loops as shown below. Glue the ends of the first strip together to make a simple loop. Do the same with the second strip, but turn one end over before gluing so that there is one twist in the strip. For the third loop, twist one end twice before you glue the ends together.*

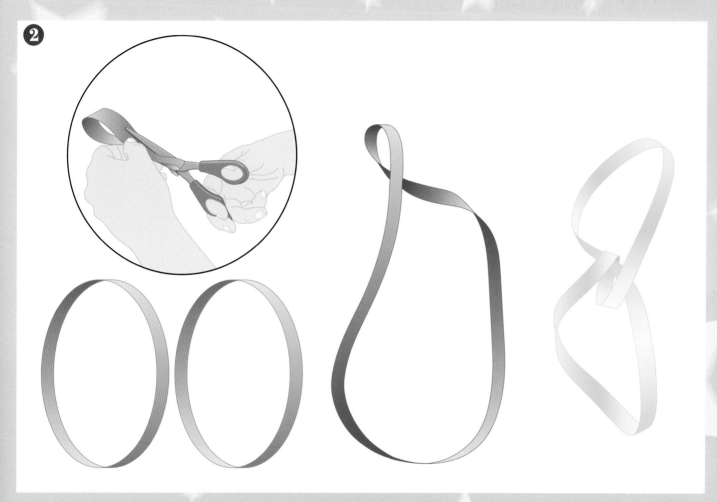

2   To perform the trick, simply cut each paper loop
    down the center. The first becomes two separate
    loops, the second becomes one large loop, and
    the third makes two loops linked together.

FLOATING ON AIR

You will need:
- *the special card supplied in the box*
- *dead matchstick, toothpick, or small piece of paper*

For over thirty years, Mercedes Talma was part of a successful triple act, but she was also an accomplished magician in her own right. In spite of the fact that she had small hands, she was an expert at coin manipulations and is regarded as one of the most famous female magicians of all time.

Talma, as she came to be known, was born Mary Ford in 1868. She married the Belgian magician Servais Le Roy in 1890, when she adopted her stage name and became part of a very successful act called Le Roy, Talma, and Bosco (Bosco was the comedy part of the act; several people took on this role between 1904 and 1930).

Many magician's assistants have appeared to defy the laws of gravity by floating in midair. Your assistant here may be a humble matchstick, but the mystery can be just as entertaining as the large-scale version.

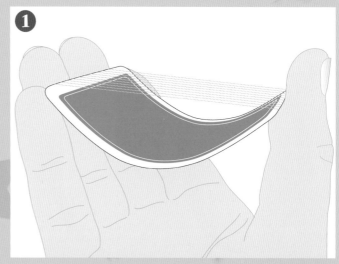

1   *If you gently bend the special card upwards at each end, you will see there are several lines of fine thread running from one end of the card to the other. You can see them close up, but they will not be visible from further away. These will enable you to perform this very baffling trick.*

42

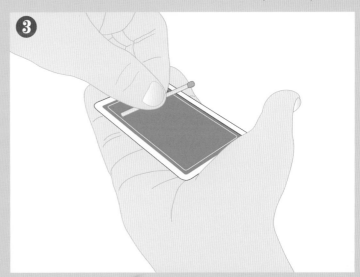

2 Place the card on the flat of the palm of your right hand.

3 Place the dead matchstick on the card across the threads (you know they are there, but they will be invisible to your audience).

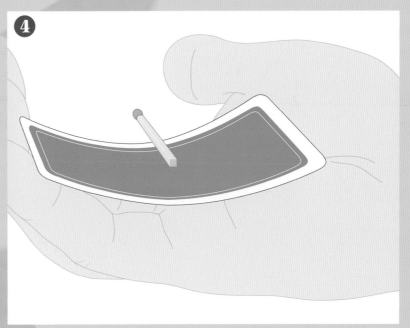

4 With your wand in your left hand, wave it above the match as if you are casting a spell. At the same time, gradually bend the base of your fingers and the base of your thumb inwards so that the card curves slightly.

   Do this bending very slowly, and the match will appear to float in the air above the card. Relax your hand, and the match will descend back onto the card.

You will need:
- *just yourself*

SHOW OF STRENGTH

Although she was of small build, no one, not even the strongest of men, could lift Annie Abbott from the floor, and she appeared superior to strong men in many other sensational feats of strength.

She was born Dixie Annie Jarratt in America in 1861, and took the stage name of Annie Abbott after watching similar feats performed by Lulu Hurst. Her first performance was in March 1885, and within a few short years she was touring major cities all over America. A successful tour in New York City led to a long run in London, followed by tours of Europe and Russia. Here is one of Annie Abbott's feats of apparent strength.

1 Tell your audience that you are stronger than the combined strength of six people. Stand facing a wall, and place your hands flat against it with your fingers pointing upwards. Your arms must be outstretched.

2 Ask a member of the audience to stand in line behind you with his or her hands on your shoulders and arms outstretched.

44

3 Ask another five people to stand in line behind the first, each with his or her outstretched hands on the shoulders of the person in front.

4 Ask everyone to push as hard as they can to see if they can pin you against the wall. As long as you can prevent the person behind you from pushing you against the wall, you will be able to resist the strength of all the others as well. Use the strength in your wrists (not your hands) to resist the push, and you will be successful.

WAVE THE FLAG

You will need:
- *a small flag*
- *colored ribbons, matching the colors of the flag*
- *a newspaper*
- *glue*

Vonetta, "the mistress of mystery," was a leading female magician in the early part of the 20th century. She was born Etta Ion in Middlesbrough, North Yorkshire, on August 14, 1878. She started her performing career as a singer and a dancer.

One of the highlights of Vonetta's act was that after each trick she would go behind a flag and emerge, almost instantly, wearing a different costume. Another was that she often featured the magical production of flags of different countries from which she produced three girls.

She retired from the stage at the beginning of the First World War, when her assistants had to go and fight for their country. She became a nurse for the duration of the war.

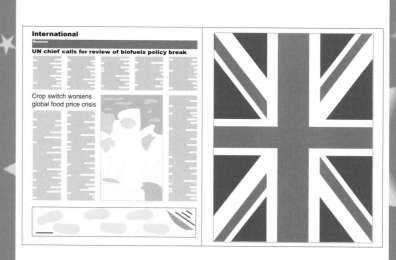

1 Open the newspaper at the center and lay the flag on the right-hand side.

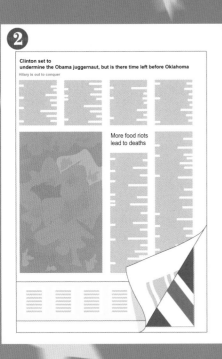

2 Place a single sheet from the same newspaper on top of the flag, and then put glue on the edges of the single sheet and glue the two pages together with the flag between them. Close the newspaper. All of this must be done in secret before your show.

3 In your act, open the newspaper and place it flat on your table. Show the ribbons and drop them on top of the newspaper.

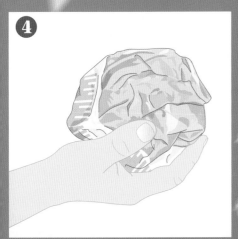

4 Pick up the secretly prepared center pages and fold them over the ribbons, making sure that the prepared page (with the hidden flag) is on top of the resulting paper ball.

5 Wave your wand over the paper ball, and then tear open the top sheet and pull out the flag. Casually drop the newspaper package onto your table or into a wastebasket as you wave the flag and take your applause.

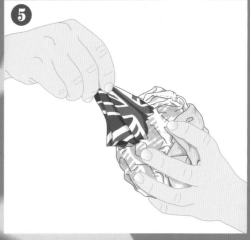

INDEX

Afghan Bands trick, 40–1

Amazing Production trick, an, 22–3

Anderson, John Henry, of Scotland, 22

Anneman, Stanley, 34

Annemann, Ted (Theodore John Squires), 34

Ball and Vase trick, 28

Cameron, Rita, 20

Cardini (Richard Valentine Pitchford), 12

Carmo (Henry Cameron), 20

Carmo's Beads trick, 20–1

Chameleon Colors trick, 24–5

Conjuring with Cards trick, 12–13

Crazy Compass trick, 16–17

Dante (August Harry Jansen), 26

De Vere, Charles, 39

Dice Deception trick, 30–1

Dictionary Test trick, the, 38

Duval, Ade, (Adolph Amrein), 24

Floating on Air trick, 42–3

Fogel, Maurice, 36

Great Wizard of the North, the, 22

Herrmann, Adelaide (born Scarcez), 40

Herrmann, Alexander, 26, 40

Herrmann, Leon, 40

Herrmann the Great, 16

Hoffmann, Professor, 36, 40

Koran, Al (Edward Doe), 30

Levante, Esme, 39

Levante, the Great, 39

Le Roy, Servais, 42

Le Roy, Talma and Bosco, 42

Looking into the Future trick, 36–7

Magic Washing trick, 26

Magician's Oath, the, 7

Malini, Max, (Max Katz Brelt), 10

Money Magic trick, 10–11

Okita (Julia Ferrett), 39

Okito (Tobias "Theo" Leendert Bamberg), 4, 14

Open Sesame trick, 34–5

Oriental Wizardry trick, 14–15

patter, 8

performing magic, 6–7

Piddington, Lesley, 32

Piddington, Sydney, 32

practice, 6, 7–8, 9

Show of Strength trick, 44–5

Talma, Mercedes (Mary Ford), 42

Telephone Telepathy trick, 32–3

Thurston, Howard, 5, 16, 24, 26

Traveling Coin trick, 18

Vonetta (Etta Ion), 46

Wave the Flag trick, 46–7